LAZY
Lunches

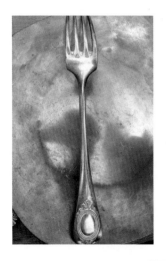

LAZY
Lunches

Marlene van der Westhuizen

BOOK**STORM**

MACMILLAN

ACKNOWLEDGEMENTS

I wrote this little book for my husband, Deon, and our son, Renier …
to use on their fabulous hunting trips.

As always there are numerous people to thank: Basil van Rooyen, Louise Grantham,
Lindsey Cohen, René de Wet, Heather Parker, as well as photographers Stephen Inggs
and Gerda Genis. Also Dawie Verwey who at really short notice produced lovely photographs for all
the new recipes. Thanks to all of you for helping to produce this little gem.

ISBN: 978-1-920434-06-9
First edition, first impression 2010

Published jointly by Bookstorm (Pty) Limited, PO Box 4532, Northcliff, 2115, Johannesburg, South Africa,
www.bookstorm.co.za
and Pan Macmillan South Africa, Private Bag X19, Northlands, 2116, Johannesburg, South Africa,
www.panmacmillan.co.za

Distributed by Pan Macmillan Via Booksite Afrika

Photography by Stephen Inggs, Gerda Genis and Dawie Verwey
Edited by Content by design
Proofread by Vanessa Perlman
Design and layout by René de Wet
Printed by Ultra Litho

Contents

Preface

The idea of a little book just for lunches, a book you can toss into your weekend bag as you grab your car keys, appealed to me the moment it was suggested. Combining the best of the lunch recipes from my previous books, *Delectable* and *Sumptuous*, made sense. Big books don't travel!

Naturally, I have added some new recipes from the storm we are cooking up at the Food Studio in Green Point, Cape Town, and at the kitchen of Bagatelle, our home in the Auvergne.

They are all in the familiar brasserie luxe style I love – food that reminds you of comfort and warmth, cosy kitchens and long summer afternoons around a table with family and friends. Enjoy the moment!

Marlene van der Westhuizen
Cape Town, 2010

Chapter 1

Under the pomegranate tree

During late January and February, we share the pomegranate tree with sunbirds and, occasionally, a mouse. The wide-open fruit in the top branches is just too tempting a feast! Over the years, we have learned the hard way to move the table slightly during this time to avoid lunching in a rain of tiny discarded pips!

These are the best days of the year ... little wind, long sun-filled days and it is quiet – most of the tourists have left. The late summer figs and apples are out, along with pears and early quinces. It is time for roasting tiny sardines with garlic and for making terrines, pâtés, cold soups and creamy pastas. A time of lightness.

Chilled tomato soup

This country-style soup combines all the typical summer flavours and ingredients that epitomise a gentle meal in the French countryside.

Liquidise all the ingredients except the yoghurt. Fold the yoghurt into the soup and season to taste. Chill for at least an hour before you serve this summery soup with a small green salad and some warm, crusty bread. I love adding a dollop of tapenade as garnish!

- 800 g slightly overripe tomatoes, skinned and seeded
- ½ cucumber, peeled and sliced
- 2 leeks, sliced in pennies, well rinsed and chopped
- 2 cloves garlic, chopped
- 4 red peppers, roasted, peeled, seeded and chopped
- 150 ml plain yoghurt
- sea salt and freshly ground black pepper to taste

Mushroom soup

Serves 6

Share this lovely soup with some good friends and enjoy with a fresh, still warm bread and, possibly, a wonderfully robust glass of wine.

- 1 T olive oil
- 2 brown onions, peeled and chopped
- 2 medium potatoes, peeled and chopped
- 750 ml rich chicken stock*
- 2 T butter
- 250 g mushrooms of your choice, chopped
- salt and freshly ground black pepper
- 3 T crème fraîche

Heat the olive oil in a smallish pot, add the onions, and fry over medium heat until translucent. Add the potatoes and chicken stock, and cook until the potatoes are soft – about 20 minutes.

In the meantime, melt the butter in a small skillet, and allow it to brown to beurre noisette stage. Add the mushrooms to the skillet and fry at high heat until most of the juice has caramelised. Tip into the pot and stir well.

Purée in a food processor until completely smooth and wonderfully glossy. Season to taste and add more stock if it is a little too thick.

Return the soup to the pot and reheat to piping hot, then ladle it into soup bowls.

Add a dollop of crème fraîche and garnish with a sliver or two of raw mushroom.

* Enrich stock by adding to one litre of chicken stock the following: 12 chicken wings, a peeled carrot or two, one celery stick, a clove or two of peeled garlic, a bouquet garni and about 500 ml water. Bring to the boil and cook until the meat comes off the bones. Pour through a sieve … and voila – the most delicious, rich stock you can imagine!

Potato, bean & prosciutto salad

This is a truly great salad to serve at a garden lunch. I pair it with some chilled Merlot. Always spectacular!

- 1 kg baby potatoes, scrubbed, boiled and kept warm
- 2 handfuls baby green beans, lightly cooked but still crunchy
- 1 bunch chives, chopped
- 6 slices prosciutto, cut into narrow strips and lightly grilled
- walnut oil to taste
- salt and freshly ground black pepper to taste

Toss the potatoes, beans, chives and prosciutto together. Drizzle with the walnut oil, season and serve immediately.

Pasta with red pepper sauce

Serves 4

This lovely pasta can be served alongside a splendid fish – and, of course, just by itself.

- 2 red peppers, grilled, seeded and peeled
- 125 ml extra virgin olive oil
- 2,5 ml each paprika, cardamon and ginger powder
- 2 cloves garlic, peeled and chopped
- salt and freshly ground black pepper
- 4 servings tagliolini
- 50 ml extra virgin olive oil
- 5 ml sea salt
- black pepper to taste

Slice the peppers roughly and place in a blender. Heat the olive oil gently in a frying pan, and lightly fry the spices and garlic. Add the mix to the peppers in the blender. Purée. Return to the pan and reheat without bringing to a boil. Season with sea salt and freshly ground black pepper.

Meanwhile, cook the tagliolini according to packet instructions until al dente. Drain, return to the warm pot and toss with the olive oil and salt.

Spoon the red pepper sauce over the warm pasta and, if you like, garnish with Parmesan shavings. Pass the pepper grinder over each plate, grinding furiously before serving!

Chicken liver pâté with port jelly

I love liver pâté, but became really bored with the slightly sludgy look! Had to change it ... this is totally great!

Port jelly
- 4 leaves gelatine
- 300 ml port

- 250 g salted butter
- 6 leeks, sliced in pennies and washed
- 500 g chicken livers
- handful thyme
- 75 ml cognac*
- salt and freshly ground black pepper
- 1 large bunch black grapes, halved and seeded

Warm the port over a low heat. Soak the gelatine leaves in cold water for a couple of minutes and then add to the port. Stir until the gelatine has melted completely. Remove from the heat.

Melt half the butter in a pan and cook the leeks until soft. Add the livers, strip the thyme and add the leaves, and cook lightly (you want the livers to still be pink on the inside). Add the cognac. Remove from the heat. Add the rest of the butter to the mixture and, using a handheld liquidiser, process the mixture until completely smooth. Season.

Spoon into a greased earthenware bowl.

Arrange the grapes on top of the pâté. Spoon the cooled port jelly over the pâté and place in the fridge overnight.

You'll end up with an utterly glamorous pre-party snack!

* Brandy will do nicely as well.

Sardines oven-roasted

A delectable way to start any lunch – especially those lazy ones outside.

- 10 ml olive oil
- 16 fresh sardines, gutted and rinsed
- 8 cloves garlic
- 5 ml Maldon sea salt
- 5 ml freshly ground black pepper

Preheat the oven to 180 deg C/Gas 4. Oil a baking tray with the olive oil, pat the sardines dry, and place them in two rows on the tray. Sprinkle the whole garlic cloves around the little fish. Gently roast the fish and garlic for about 15 minutes. It is not necessary to turn them over.

Remove the tray from the oven, season the beauties with salt and freshly ground black pepper, and serve them immediately with a crisp green salad and a glass of Sauvignon Blanc.

Fromage de chèvre tartlets

I love sharing gems like these little tarts with my fabulous friends under our ancient pomegranate tree.

- 1 roll puff pastry, thawed
- 50 ml butter
- 3 onions, peeled and sliced in rings
- 15 ml fresh thyme, chopped
- 6 medium-sized Rosa tomatoes, sliced
- 1 chèvre, cut in even rounds
- 3 salad onions, chopped

Preheat the oven to 220 deg C/Gas 7. Line 6 loose-bottomed tartlet pans with puff pastry. It is not necessary to thin the pastry – use it as it is, quite thick.

Melt the butter in a small pot and fry the onion rings until they are transparent. Add the thyme and cook for 5 minutes, making sure the onions don't burn. Remove from the heat and let it cool a bit. Divide between the pastry cases. Place three slices of tomato in each tart, on top of the onion. Place a slice of chèvre right on top. Bake for 10 minutes or until the pastry is crisp and golden. Sprinkle with the chopped salad onions, and serve with a light green salad as a starter. This is so good in summer …

(To make sure the bottom of the pastry is not soggy, brush with a little egg white and pre-bake empty for 2 minutes. It works really well …)

Terrine de campagne

- 20 g butter plus extra for greasing the terrine dish
- 125 g mushrooms, chopped
- 250 g bacon, cut in tiny slivers
- 2 onions, chopped
- pinch powdered cloves
- pinch grated nutmeg
- 2 t fresh thyme, chopped
- 2 t fresh sage, chopped
- 225 g pork loin, cut in tiny cubes
- 225 g veal, cut in cubes
- 225 g chicken liver
- 3 cloves garlic, crushed
- 150 ml cognac or good-quality brandy
- 2 large eggs, whisked
- 125 ml cream
- sea salt and freshly ground black pepper
- bacon strips, enough to line a 2 ℓ terrine dish
- 225 g chicken breast, fried in 1 T olive oil with 3 sage leaves, and cut into thin slices
- 225 g smoked ham or pancetta, cut into thin slices

Melt 10 g butter until it is golden and gives off a nutty smell (the beurre noisette stage). Fry the mushrooms until they are beautifully caramelised and cooked fairly dry. Then scoop from the pan and set aside. Add the rest of the butter to the pan and melt. Fry the bacon slivers and onions until the onions are translucent and the bacon quite crispy. Add the cloves, nutmeg, thyme and sage. Spoon half of the mushrooms and half of the bacon-onion mix into a food processor, and put the remaining halves of the mushrooms and bacon-onion mix into a mixing bowl.

Add the pork loin and veal to the mixing bowl with the mushrooms and bacon-onion mix.

Gently fry the liver with the garlic in the leftover pan juices until cooked but still pink on the inside. Add the cognac, bring to a fast boil and flambée. Spoon half of the liver and all the juices into the food processor to join the mushrooms and bacon-onion mix already in it. Process until smooth. Add the eggs and the cream, and process again. Season.

Cut the remaining liver into small cubes. Add to the rest of the ingredients in the mixing bowl, spoon the purée from the food processor into the bowl, and fold together to form a rough paste. Taste and season if needed. Preheat the oven to 180 deg C/Gas 4. Grease the terrine dish with butter, and line with the bacon strips,

continues overleaf

allowing them to fall over the sides of the dish.

Spoon half the mixture into the terrine dish and arrange the slices of chicken and ham or pancetta on top. Add the rest of the purée and level perfectly. Fold the bacon over the filling to cover.

Cover the terrine dish with greased foil and put in a bain-marie in the oven for about 90 minutes. Remove from the oven and allow to cool. Remove the foil, put some waxed paper on top and weigh down – a couple of tins from the store cupboard work really well!

Remove the weights after about 2 hours and place the terrine in the fridge for at least 2 days to allow the flavours to marry. To remove from the terrine dish, dip the whole dish in warm water for a second or two, gently pry the edges loose with a sharp knife, and tip onto a platter or cutting board.

Enjoy with a glass of Pinot Noir.

Small mackerel & sweet potato fishcakes

Simple but really special is the best way to describe these little bite-size fishcakes.

- 1 large sweet potato
- olive oil
- 3 peppered mackerel fillets
- zest of 2 lemons
- 125 g Parmesan, grated
- sea salt and freshly ground black pepper
- 200 g rocket leaves
- sweet chilli sauce to use as a dip

Preheat the oven to 180 deg C/Gas 4. Peel and cube the sweet potato. Place in an ovenproof dish with a splash of olive oil and a small amount of water (just enough to form a film at the base of the dish). Cover and steam until tender. Drain and allow to cool.

Remove the skins from the mackerel fillets. Roughly flake the fillets into a mixing bowl. Add the lemon zest. Mash and fold into the sweet potato, adding the Parmesan. Taste, and season with salt and pepper if required.

Mould the mixture into small fishcakes. If the mixture is too moist, add a tiny bit of flour.

Gently fry in a small amount of olive oil and then place in the hot oven to heat it through.

Serve with rocket leaves and sweet chilli sauce.

Chapter 2

In the Green Point Village garden

I wake to the harsh sound of hadedas kicking up a racket in the plum tree. They drown the more soothing sound of the fountain and the rhythmic clicking of the frogs in the pond. I love my real city garden in the heart of Green Point Village, just a spit away from my favourite deli, Giovannis, where I often head when I plan a patio lunch.

I'll pick up sorrel for the soup, buffalo mozzarella for the salad, a lovely shiny aubergine and a handful of baby tomatoes. City living can be really good.

Creamy sweet potato & thyme soup

This is a truly creamy, comforting soup. The combined flavour of sweet potato and thyme is hugely satisfying.

- 50 ml extra virgin olive oil
- 5 cloves garlic, peeled and sliced
- 1 large onion, diced
- 1 celery stick, diced
- 1 red chilli, diced
- 1 kg sweet potatoes, peeled and diced
- 6 sprigs thyme
- 1 *l* chicken stock
- 150 ml double cream
- seasoning
- extra cream and thyme for garnishing

Gently heat the olive oil in a flameproof saucepan. Fry the garlic lightly until it becomes a light caramel colour. Add the onion, celery and chilli and fry until soft.

Add the sweet potatoes and keep tossing until all the pieces are coated with the oil and onion mixture. Add the thyme and stock, and simmer for about 20 minutes or until soft.

Remove the thyme, purée the soup in a liquidiser and return to the saucepan. Reheat, stir in the cream, season and serve immediately. Garnish with a dollop of cream and a sprig of thyme. Lovely!

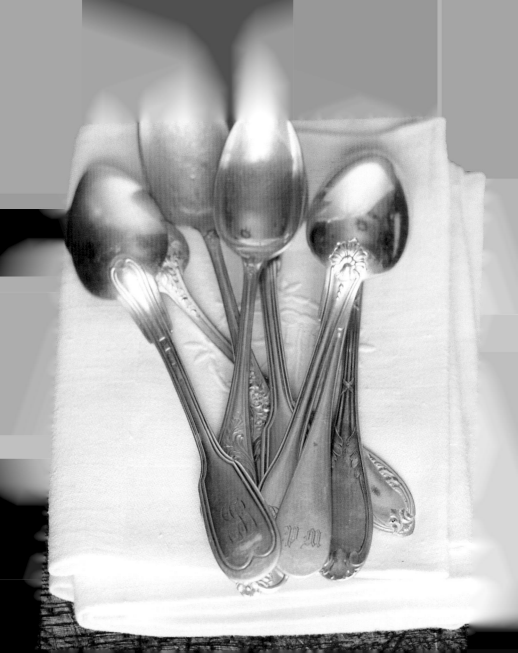

Spinach & sorrel soup

Undeniably one of the prettier soups I've seen. And healthier than most.

- 75 ml olive oil
- 5 medium leeks, sliced into pennies and washed
- 2 cloves garlic, chopped
- 600 g baby spinach leaves, washed
- 300 g sorrel leaves, washed
- 1 ½ ℓ chicken stock
- salt and freshly ground black pepper to taste
- 150 ml crème fraîche
- 3 t horseradish cream
- salt and freshly ground black pepper to taste

Heat the olive oil in a large pot, add the leeks and cook until they are translucent and meltingly soft. Add the garlic, still-wet spinach and sorrel, and steam gently until the leaves have wilted. Add a little chicken stock – about 100 ml should be fine. Spoon everything into a food processor and whizz to a thinnish purée. Pour it back into the pot, add the rest of the stock, stir well and bring to a gentle simmer. Season.

In a little mixing bowl, fold the crème fraîche and the horseradish cream together.

Ladle the soup into individual soup bowls, garnish with a dollop of the creamy mixture and serve immediately.

Bouquet garni

- 1 leek
- 1 sprig oregano
- 5 sprigs rosemary
- 1 thin celery stick, 8 cm long
- 2 bay leaves
- 1 piece string, 12 cm long

Trim the bottom of the leek and remove the two outer leaves by cutting them lengthwise. Rinse well. Fold all the herbs, including the celery, into the first leek leaf. Fold the second one over the open end of the first. Fold the 2 bay leaves around the parcel and tie with the piece of string. Add the bouquet garni to any pot-au-feu or daube and taste the difference!

Caprese salad

This is a classic recipe – I'm serving it in a fresh way, which really highlights the way it works. Use the best olive oil you can find.

- 2 ripe tomatoes, each sliced into 6 rounds
- sea salt and freshly ground black pepper
- 1 round of buffalo mozzarella, sliced … cut the edges off, sprinkle some salt and olive oil on them and eat quickly when no-one's looking
- basil, freshly chopped
- 100 ml extra virgin olive oil

Salt the tomato slices individually. Salt and pepper the mozzarella slices and let them rest.

Take 4 plates and place 3 tomato slices on each.

Sprinkle the basil over the tomatoes. Place the mozzarella slices in a little stack next to the tomatoes.

Pour 25 ml olive oil in each of 4 tot glasses and put a glass on each plate, next to the cheese.

Serve with crusty white bread.

Aubergine caviar

Serves about 6 as a dip for crudités

I enjoy watching this lovely dip disappearing – always a hit!

- 2 medium aubergines, whole
- 2 T olive oil
- 3 cloves garlic, peeled and chopped
- 4 salad onions, finely chopped
- juice of 1 lemon
- 2 T flat-leaf parsley, chopped
- 250 ml crème fraîche
- sea salt and freshly ground black pepper to taste

Prick the aubergines all over with a fork and rub them with olive oil before roasting them at about 200 deg C/Gas 6 for 15 to 20 minutes, until completely tender. Remove from the oven, let them cool a bit ... for obvious reasons ... then cut in half and scoop the flesh into a mixing bowl. Add the garlic, salad onions, lemon juice, parsley and crème fraîche and gently fold together. Season to taste and serve with freshly sliced crudités.

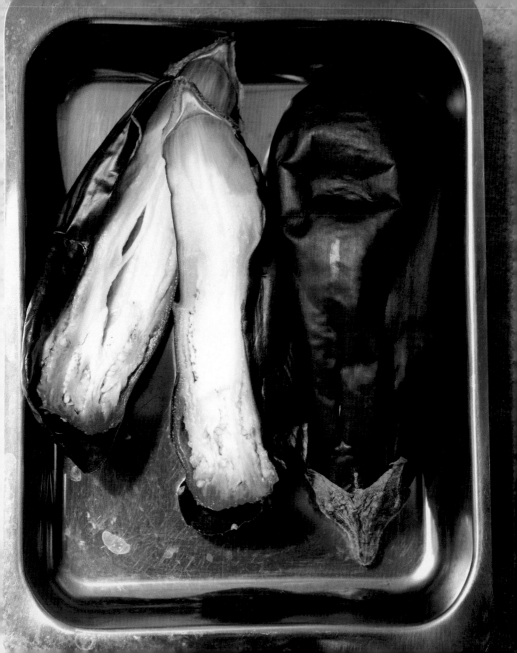

Goat's cheese tarts with hazelnuts

A great starter to kick off with.

- 25 ml olive oil
- 5 young leeks, sliced into pennies and well-rinsed
- 4 sprigs thyme, chopped
- 1 roll puff pastry
- 1 egg yolk, slightly beaten
- 6 slices goat's cheese
- handful wild rocket
- 50 g hazelnuts, roasted and peeled
- 50 ml hazelnut oil

Preheat the oven to 220 deg C/Gas 7. Heat the olive oil in a saucepan, add the leeks and thyme, and simmer gently, covered, for about 20 minutes, until the leeks are soft. Remove the lid, increase the heat, reduce the liquid, and cook until the leeks are slightly caramelised.

Using a cutter, punch 6 rounds out of the pastry and place them on a greased baking tray. Chill for about 10 minutes. Brush each round with a little egg yolk before spooning a dollop of leeks onto the middle of each round, leaving a border. Top with a slice of goat's cheese. Chill for 10 more minutes before baking for about 15 minutes in the hot oven.

Season lightly, and serve with rocket, a sprinkling of nuts and a dash of hazelnut oil.

Baked red peppers with baby tomatoes

If you ever need to cater for a vegan, leave out the anchovies – this is also a fantastic main course. Accompany it with a really good wine.

- 4 red peppers
- 75 ml extra virgin olive oil
- 2 leeks, diced and washed
- 6 anchovies
- 20 baby tomatoes
- 250 ml basil leaves, chopped
- 3 cloves garlic, finely chopped
- salt and freshly ground black pepper

Preheat the oven to 200 deg C/Gas 6. Lightly oil a large, shallow baking pan. Halve the red peppers lengthwise and clean out the seeds and pith. Arrange the peppers, open ends up, in the pan.

Add 20 ml olive oil to a frying pan, heat it gently and sauté the leeks in the oil until translucent. Add the anchovies and stir the mixture until the anchovies have melted. Remove from the heat. Halve the tomatoes lengthwise and toss in a bowl with the basil and garlic.

Fold the leek mixture into the tomato and basil mixture and toss well. Add the rest of the oil, salt and freshly ground black pepper to taste.

Divide the mixture between the peppers and roast in the hot oven until the peppers are tender, between 15 and 20 minutes. Serve as a starter with a handful of rocket per plate and a basil leaf for garnish.

For a change, replace the leek and anchovy mixture with a spoonful of tapenade in each pepper – a very zesty taste!

Potato & paprika bake

This recipe hails from a family friend, Maria Mayer, and has become an all-round favourite.

- 2 T extra virgin olive oil
- 6 green peppers, seeded and sliced in rings
- 6 large onions, peeled and sliced in rings
- 5 cloves garlic, peeled and chopped
- 250 g bacon, cut into small strips
- 12 large waxy potatoes, cooked and peeled
- sea salt and freshly ground black pepper
- 12 eggs, hard-boiled, peeled and sliced
- 2 T paprika
- 375 ml fresh cream

Warm half the olive oil in a large pot. Combine the peppers, onions, garlic and bacon, and fry until the onions are translucent and the bacon just crisp. Oil an ovenproof dish with the rest of the olive oil. Slice the potatoes into thin rings and place a layer on the bottom of the dish. Dust with seasoning. Spoon a layer of the vegetable and bacon mixture on top of the potatoes. Add a layer of egg. Sprinkle liberally with paprika. Repeat until you have used all the ingredients, finishing with a layer of egg.

Pour the cream over the dish and bake, covered, for 45 minutes at 180 deg C/Gas 4. This is excellent served with red meat.

Provençal vegetable tart

Served with a green salad, this is going to be very popular among your friends.

- 1 onion
- 1 courgette
- 1 small aubergine
- olive oil
- 6 cherry tomatoes, halved
- 6 sundried tomatoes in oil, chopped
- 1 bunch basil
- 10 black olives
- 250 g puff pastry
- salt and freshly ground black pepper

Preheat the oven to 180 deg C/Gas 4. Peel and slice the onion and cut the courgette and aubergine into small cubes. Sauté all of the vegetables in the olive oil, keeping them al dente. Pick off the basil leaves, dress them in olive oil and stone the olives. Roll out the pastry, cover with all of the vegetables and herbs, and season. Cook in the oven for 30 minutes.

On the Food Studio stoep

Chapter 3

After a hard week's cooking and serving, with a catering fridge full of delicious leftovers and produce, it is a perfect time to invite friends for a casual lunch at the Karoo-slate table. We stack all the half-bottles of wine on a tray at the end of the table, haul out the tasting glasses and start to cook ... A wonderful vintner's soup, red peppers stuffed with tuna, a French-style pizza with anchovies and tomatoes, and chicken livers with prosciutto. A variety of fun dishes to be shared with family and friends. The easy life.

La soupe des vendanges

This French winemaker's soup provides great comfort after a long day's work.

- 4 T extra virgin olive oil
- 4 leeks, sliced in pennies and washed
- 2 medium carrots, peeled and sliced in pennies
- 4 medium potatoes, peeled and sliced
- 250 g haricot beans
- 4 cloves garlic, peeled and chopped
- 350 g pork belly, diced
- 1 shoulder of springbok, whole with bone
- 3 × 10 cm marrow bones – ask your butcher!
- 1 fattened duck
- 2 bottles of dry white wine
- 2 ℓ water
- bouquet garni
- salt and freshly ground black pepper

For this soup, I use the biggest pot I can lay my hands on – in Charroux, it's usually the ancient Rosieres I found in a brocante in a village close to Vichy; in the Cape, a little more prosaic, it's a 24 ℓ I bought from the local chef's shop.

Heat the olive oil and gently braise the leeks, carrots, potatoes, beans, garlic and pork belly until the leeks are translucent but not browned. Add the springbok, marrow bones and duck to the pot. Cover with the wine and water, and bring to the boil. Reduce the heat to a simmer and add the bouquet garni.

After about 2 hours, you can remove the venison, duck and marrow bones from the pot and debone the meat. I use my fingers (after the meat has cooled down a little!) to shred the meat in smallish pieces before returning it to the soup. At this point, you can skim some fat from the soup. Allow the soup to reduce enough to be fairly thick, season and then serve it in hearty portions with a dollop of aioli and a warm, crusty slice of bread.

La soupe des vendanges

This French winemaker's soup provides great comfort after a long day's work.

- 4 T extra virgin olive oil
- 4 leeks, sliced in pennies and washed
- 2 medium carrots, peeled and sliced in pennies
- 4 medium potatoes, peeled and sliced
- 250 g haricot beans
- 4 cloves garlic, peeled and chopped
- 350 g pork belly, diced
- 1 shoulder of springbok, whole with bone
- 3 × 10 cm marrow bones – ask your butcher!
- 1 fattened duck
- 2 bottles of dry white wine
- 2 ℓ water
- bouquet garni
- salt and freshly ground black pepper

For this soup, I use the biggest pot I can lay my hands on – in Charroux, it's usually the ancient Rosieres I found in a brocante in a village close to Vichy; in the Cape, a little more prosaic, it's a 24 ℓ I bought from the local chef's shop.

Heat the olive oil and gently braise the leeks, carrots, potatoes, beans, garlic and pork belly until the leeks are translucent but not browned. Add the springbok, marrow bones and duck to the pot. Cover with the wine and water, and bring to the boil. Reduce the heat to a simmer and add the bouquet garni.

After about 2 hours, you can remove the venison, duck and marrow bones from the pot and debone the meat. I use my fingers (after the meat has cooled down a little!) to shred the meat in smallish pieces before returning it to the soup. At this point, you can skim some fat from the soup. Allow the soup to reduce enough to be fairly thick, season and then serve it in hearty portions with a dollop of aioli and a warm, crusty slice of bread.

Butternut & leek soup

A lovely soup to enjoy with family or friends.

- 50 g butter
- 6 leeks, sliced in pennies and washed thoroughly
- 1 kg sliced butternut
- 1 ℓ chicken stock
- 2 cloves garlic, chopped
- 5 g nutmeg, grated
- sea salt and freshly ground black pepper
- crème fraîche
- sage, to garnish

Melt the butter in a large pot. Fry the leeks lightly until soft and translucent. Add the butternut to the pot and toss. Fry lightly.

Pour the chicken stock over the vegetables and bring to a gentle boil. Turn down the heat and simmer until the butternut is completely cooked and tender. Add the garlic and nutmeg.

Remove the pot from the heat. Using a handheld liquidiser, whizz until it reaches a completely creamy consistency. Season to taste.

Serve in individual soup bowls, with a dollop of crème fraîche spooned onto each serving. Garnish each with a sage leaf.

Chicken livers with prosciutto & roasted baby potato salad

Serves 6

This feeds my addiction to sage ...

- small knob of butter
- 100 g prosciutto, sliced in ribbons
- 3 leeks, sliced in pennies and washed
- 500 g chicken livers, cleaned
- 25 ml brandy
- 50 ml olive oil
- 12 small potatoes, washed and boiled until just tender
- 20 sage leaves

Heat the butter in a small pan and quick-fry the prosciutto until crisp.

Remove from the pan. Pat the leeks dry and fry till they are soft and lightly cooked. Remove from the pan and add the livers. Cook the livers lightly, taking care not to overcook – it's best if the livers are still slightly pink on the inside. Add the brandy to the pan, bring to a fast boil and toss a burning match in its direction. Don't panic if the entire pan catches fire ... it's what you want! Remove the pan from the heat (the flames will die away soon enough).

Spoon the livers onto a dish and add the prosciutto and leeks.

Add the olive oil to the pan juices. Reheat. Slice the potatoes and add them to the pan. Cook until they are heated through. Add the sage leaves to the pan and warm. Toss the potatoes and sage into the dish with the livers, prosciutto and leeks, and serve!

Tomato tarts

For a refreshing change, make a single tart using a large flan dish. Use exactly the same method and ingredients. Just adjust the amount of tomatoes in order to fill the dish completely.

- 1 sheet puff pastry, thawed
- 2 leeks, chopped and lightly sautéed in butter
- 125 g Roquefort cheese, sliced
- 100 ml egg mayonnaise
- 30 red cherry tomatoes

Preheat the oven to 220 deg C/Gas 7. Cut the pastry into rounds that will fit snugly into greased loose-bottomed flan dishes. Prick the bases with a fork and divide the fried leeks between them. Place a slice of cheese on each layer of leeks. Spoon a small dollop of mayonnaise on top of the cheese, and follow that with five whole tomatoes for each tart.

Bake the tarts in the preheated oven for about 20 minutes. The puff pastry will rise beautifully around the filling and become a caramel colour.

Serve straight from the oven with a crisp salad.

Red peppers with tuna

It seems like an odd combination, but the sweetness of the peppers and the meatiness of the tuna make for a surprisingly satisfying – but light – summer lunch.

- 3 red peppers, halved lengthwise and seeded
- 60 ml olive oil
- sea salt and freshly ground black pepper
- 250 g fresh tuna fillet
- zest and juice of 1 lemon
- 1 small green chilli, seeded and chopped
- 1 teaspoon fresh oregano, chopped

Brush the peppers with some of the olive oil and cook under the grill until soft. Set aside. Season the tuna and pan-fry over a high heat in olive oil, turning once. Chill and slice into small cubes.

Chop the zest, set some aside, and mix the rest with the lemon juice, chilli, oregano and the rest of the olive oil. Add the tuna and toss. Fill the pepper halves with the mixture, sprinkle with reserved zest and serve on rocket.

Pissaladière

Pastry
- 500 g plain flour
- ¼ t salt
- 125 g cold unsalted butter, cubed
- 2 eggs, beaten

Topping
- 6 shallots, peeled and chopped
- 4 cloves garlic, chopped
- 8 small courgettes, sliced in pennies
- 8 red tomatoes, sliced quite thickly
- 20 red or yellow baby tomatoes, halved and slightly oven-dried
- 10 tiny purple artichokes, cooked and halved*
- handful of fresh herbs such as basil, rosemary, thyme and sage, chopped
- salt and freshly ground black pepper to taste
- 20 anchovy fillets
- 250 g grated hard cheese (Cantal, Parmesan)
- extra virgin olive oil

Make the pastry first: pulse the flour with the salt in a food processor. Add the butter, and pulse until the mixture resembles coarse breadcrumbs. Add the eggs and pulse until the dough begins to form a mass.

Transfer to a work surface and gather in a ball. Using the palm of your hand, flatten into a disc, wrap in plastic and refrigerate for about 2 hours, until chilled.

Roll out on a lightly floured surface to form a rectangle about 32 cm × 40 cm and about 5 mm thick.

Transfer to a large baking sheet. Refrigerate again until the dough is firm ... 10 minutes should be enough.

Now set the oven to 190 deg C/Gas 5. Scatter the shallots, garlic and courgettes over the pastry base.

Arrange the sliced tomatoes in slightly overlapping rows inside the rim of the dough. Fill any gaps with the baby tomatoes and artichokes. Season with the herbs, salt and pepper. Decorate with the anchovies. Sprinkle with the cheese and olive oil.

Bake for 30 minutes in the top half of the oven. Then move the baking sheet down a notch and bake for another 25 minutes, or until the base is crispy. Let the pissaladière cool and cut into squares. Serve warm.

*   These delightful little artichokes are available at the fresh produce markets around Charroux during April and May. They are virtually chokeless and just about bite-sized. If you can't lay your hands on any, use bottled artichokes, but quarter them into more manageable bits.*

Salade Niçoise

The first dish I eat whenever I set foot on French soil. Delicious!

- 300 g tuna in spring water
- 18 marinated anchovies
- 30 black olives
- 6 hard-boiled eggs, cut in wedges
- 1 red capsicum, sliced in rings
- 6 tomatoes, cut into wedges
- 200 g baby green beans, lightly cooked
- 1 red onion, cut in rings
- 12 small potatoes boiled in their jackets, halved
- olive oil
- sea salt and freshly ground black pepper

These are the essential ingredients of a Parisienne salade Niçoise. Plate it and add a proper amount of olive oil, a little sea salt and freshly ground black pepper. Enjoy with a glass of crispy white wine …

Chapter 4

On the Victorian balcony

Lunch on the Victorian balcony, looking into the trees around us, is a special delight to be saved for weekends. We cook downstairs, pack trays with heaped platters and climb the huge old staircase, hefting deliciousness with us. Usually we manage to fit a weekend newspaper or two under an arm. Chilled avocado soup or melanzane Parmigiana, watermelon with feta and black olives, or a tomato, chickpea and lentil soup. Lovely food for a lazy afternoon.

Classic quiche Lorraine

We all need a quiche recipe, and this one is completely perfect.

- butter for greasing the pie dish
- 1 roll puff pastry, thawed
- 25 g butter
- 350 g bacon, cut into tiny strips
- 4 eggs
- 350 ml fresh cream
- 6 T Gruyère, grated
- handful chives, finely chopped
- salt and freshly ground black pepper

Preheat the oven to 180 deg C/Gas 4. Line a buttered pie dish with the pastry. Prick the pastry lightly with a fork and keep cold. Melt the butter in a pan and lightly fry the bacon strips until they are slightly browned. Beat together the eggs, cream, grated Gruyère and chives. Fold in the bacon, taste and then add a little salt if necessary. Grind some pepper into the mixture.

Pour into the waiting pie dish and bake for about 40 minutes. Serve with a small green salad and a glass of chilled Pinot Noir.

Tomato, chickpea & lentil soup

*What a delicious soup in which
to drown your sorrows. It was put
together by my friend, René, and is
splendid accompanied by a good
white wine.*

- 1 T olive oil
- 1 brown onion, peeled and
  chopped
- 250 g red beans, cooked
- 250 g lentils, cooked
- 250 g chickpeas, cooked
- 500 g tomatoes, peeled and
  chopped
- 1 carrot, peeled and sliced in
  pennies
- 2 cloves garlic, chopped
- 2 *l* chicken stock
- salt and freshly ground black
  pepper
- 2 T fresh parsley, chopped

Heat the olive oil in a large soup pot and lightly brown the onion before adding the beans, lentils and chickpeas. Give the vegetables a minute or two to braise gently in the olive oil before adding the tomatoes and carrot. Add the garlic and the stock and bring to a soft simmer. Boil the soup for about 10 minutes before removing it from the heat.

Pour half the soup into a food processor and pulse until it is completely smooth and creamy. Return to the pot and stir into the rest of the soup.

Heat and season before serving with a generous helping of freshly chopped parsley.

Avocado soup

On a warm summer day, this is what you want to enjoy as a cool, soothing starter.

- 2 tins good-quality chicken soup
- 3 ripe avocados
- 1 ℓ Bulgarian yoghurt
- 1 onion, finely chopped
- 125 ml cream
- 1 lemon, juiced
- seasoning

Decant the uncooked soup from the tins. Peel the avocados, remove the pips, and pop the soft meat of the avocados into a liquidiser with the yoghurt and onion. Blend. Fold the chicken soup into the mixture. Blend again until smooth, and pour into a mixing bowl. Slowly fold the cream into the mixture. Add the lemon juice to taste. Season and serve in individual bowls with a dollop of yoghurt as garnish.

Buffalo mozzarella with tomato

Serves 6

*One of my favourite salads ...
one that with a little tweaking can
always be different ... and the
same!*

- 1 T extra virgin olive oil
- 20 small Rosa tomatoes, halved
- sea salt and freshly ground black pepper
- some sprigs of thyme
- 2 fresh buffalo mozzarella*
- 20 small basil leaves
- 1 T capers

Preheat the oven to 180 deg C/Gas 4. Coat an oven pan with olive oil, toss in the tomatoes, and roast for about 30 minutes. Season lightly and set aside.

Remove the thyme leaves from their stalks and toss in with the tomatoes. Using your fingers, shred the buffalo mozzarella onto a serving platter and tuck in the basil leaves. Spoon the tomatoes and capers over the salad and enjoy with a glass of Sauvignon Blanc.

* Any other mozzarella might let you down a little ...

Melanzane Parmigiana

Serves 8

A friend, Peter Borain, makes one of the best melanzane dishes I know.

- 3 medium aubergines
- 125 ml olive oil plus extra for greasing dish and frying onion
- 1 onion, peeled and finely chopped
- 2 large cloves garlic, crushed
- 120 ml flat-leaf parsley, finely chopped
- 1 T dried oregano
- 6 really ripe tomatoes, peeled
- 25 ml tomato paste
- salt and freshly ground black pepper
- 250 g thinly sliced mozzarella*
- 250 ml basil leaves, chopped
- 100 g Parmesan, grated
- 400 ml cream

Preheat the oven to 180 deg C/Gas 4. Slice the aubergines lengthwise in thickish slices. If they are fresh, as they should be, you do not have to go through the whole 'salt and drain' process! Do not peel. Fry in the olive oil until fully cooked and soft, and put aside.

Fry the onion in a medium pot until soft and translucent. Add the garlic, parsley and oregano and fry over a low heat for no more than 2 minutes. Take care not to burn the garlic. Add the tomatoes, tomato paste, a little salt and black pepper, cover and cook gently for about 35 minutes. If you find that you have excess moisture, remove the lid and turn up the heat a little to allow the liquid to reduce.

Use a baking dish with sides at least 60 mm high. Oil the dish using a little olive oil to prevent sticking, and cover the bottom with a layer of aubergine. Follow with a layer of mozzarella, then basil and finally a layer of tomato sauce. Repeat until you run out of either ingredients or dish! The final layer is a generous sprinkle of Parmesan.

Bake for about 40 minutes. Cut in portions, spoon into small bowls, add a generous helping of cream to each serving and return to the oven for another 4 minutes. Serve immediately.

This is fantastic with a green salad.

* *Peter prefers to use buffalo mozzarella, but if you can't find any, use what you have.*

Watermelon with feta & small black olives

- 1 small and sweet watermelon, peeled and cut into bite-sized pieces
- handful fresh mint leaves
- 250 g feta
- 250 g small black olives

Gently toss the watermelon pieces and mint leaves on a large serving platter. Crumble the feta over the mixture and top with the olives. This is a delicious salad to serve in summer.

Grilled calamari with chilli & lime

- 6 cloves garlic, peeled
- 25 g fresh coriander
- 6 small green chillies
- 2 t castor sugar
- juice of 3 limes
- salt to taste
- 750 g fresh calamari
- olive oil
- extra coriander to garnish

Purée the garlic, coriander and chillies until they form a smooth paste (scrape the seeds out of the chillies for a milder bite or use less). In a bowl, mix the purée with the castor sugar and lime juice. Mix well until the sugar dissolves, and season to taste.

Clean the calamari, open the tubes and scrape out any remaining innards. Cut the tubes and tentacles into large, easy-to-eat pieces. Quickly grill the calamari in a hot pan with a little olive oil, making sure not to overcook it.

Place all the calamari on a serving dish, toss with the purée, garnish with coriander and serve immediately.

Chapter 5

In the Food Studio
kitchen

This is where I work. Every weekday and some weekends, this is the hub of my world. Deliveries of wine, meat, fish, mushrooms, piles of jewel-coloured vegetables and flowers file through the huge grey front door of the Food Studio and make it onto the thick marble slab, ready to be transformed into fabulous meals. We feed businesspeople, wine fundis and food lovers. We have groups of people attending cooking classes and wine tastings. We help make birthday parties, anniversaries and weddings magical! There is little a feast of delectable food cannot do.

Chicken & mushroom soup

On occasion, I've used guinea fowl or pheasant instead of chicken ... it's superb.

Stock

- 100 ml extra virgin olive oil
- 1 free-range chicken, ready for the pot
- 3 leeks, washed and chopped
- 1 large carrot, peeled and chopped roughly
- 4 cloves garlic, peeled and chopped
- 2 ℓ water
- 1 bouquet garni

Soup

- 2 chicken legs and 4 thighs, from the stock you've made
- 50 ml olive oil
- 150 g peeled and diced mixed turnips, carrots and sweet potatoes
- 1,5 ℓ chicken stock
- 1 t butter
- 250 g mushroom, cut in thin slivers
- seasoning
- 125 ml thick cream to garnish

Stock

Heat the olive oil in a flameproof stockpot and lightly brown the chicken carcass. Add the vegetables to the pot and sauté until softened. Add the water and bouquet garni, and bring to the boil. Keep an eye on the pot, and skim the stock regularly to remove any foam. After about an hour, when the meat starts coming off the bone, remove the carcass and strain the stock through a sieve. Keep the legs and thighs to use in the soup.

Soup

Debone the chicken legs and thighs and shred the meat. Heat the olive oil in a saucepan and lightly stir the vegetables in the oil. Pour the stock over and bring to the boil. Simmer for about 15 minutes, until the vegetables are soft. In a pan, melt the butter and fry the mushrooms until they are browned properly. Add the shredded meat and the mushrooms to the soup. Season, and spoon into large bowls, distributing the vegetables, meat and mushrooms evenly. Serve with a dollop of thick cream ... and lots of black pepper.

Carpaccio of beef or venison

Anyone with a hunter in the family needs to know about this one. It's a wow, and it's instant!

- 325 ml extra virgin olive oil
- 5 ml coriander seeds
- 5 ml paprika
- 5 ml dried sage
- 2,5 ml sea salt
- freshly ground black pepper
- 1 fillet of beef or venison (about 300 g from the chunkiest bit of the fillet)
- 50 ml capers, chopped
- 150 g Parmesan, grated
- rocket

Heat 125 ml olive oil in a saucepan and lightly fry the coriander, paprika, sage, salt and pepper. Add the fillet to the pan and quickly seal on all sides. Remove the meat to a sheet of plastic wrap, pour over most of the frying liquid, and wrap lightly.

Freeze until needed. Since the meat needs to defrost a little, remove the fillet from the freezer 20 minutes before you plan to slice the meat. Drizzle a serving platter with olive oil. Slice the fillet extremely thinly, placing each slice on the serving platter.

After each layer, season the meat, sprinkle capers and Parmesan over, and pour on more olive oil. Repeat until all the meat has been layered on the platter. You can also do individual servings. Serve with a handful of fresh, green rocket per person.

Lovely!

Pasta with tomatoes & basil

Everyone should have a quick, trusted little pasta dish in their repertoire for a really pleasant, fast meal ... this is mine.

- 200 ml extra virgin olive oil
- 400 g cherry tomatoes, whole
- 40 basil leaves, plus a few extra for garnish
- 4 servings tagliolini
- sea salt and freshly ground black pepper

Heat the olive oil in a pot and braise the tomatoes in the oil. They will swell gently and some will burst the skin, creating a very flavourful olive and tomato sauce. Do not stir. Take off the heat. Shred the basil leaves and stir them into the tomato and olive oil just before serving.

In the meantime, boil the pasta in salted water until cooked. Drain and divide into pasta bowls. Spoon the olive oil, basil and tomato mixture over, season and garnish with a whole basil leaf or two. Serve with crusty bread.

Red pepper, black olive & anchovy compote

This compote is a great starter and has its origins somewhere in the south of France. I love to serve it with warm, crusty bread and a glass of Sauvignon Blanc.

- 4 red peppers
- 125 ml extra virgin olive oil
- 250 g black olives, stoned
- 4 cloves garlic, peeled
- 10 sprigs thyme, chopped
- 20 anchovies
- 8 mint leaves
- 20 g basil leaves
- freshly ground black pepper

Grill the red peppers, turning them regularly, until the skin has blackened. Remove, let cool and skin. Remove the seeds and thinly slice the peppers. Try to catch the piquant juices … never rinse the peppers to get rid of the seeds. That's a punishable offence!

Heat the olive oil in a casserole, and stir in the peppers and olives. Add the garlic and thyme, and cook gently over a low heat for 10 minutes to infuse the flavours.

Add the anchovies, turn up the heat slightly, and stir until the anchovies have melted away. Remove from the heat. Chop the mint and basil leaves, and add.

Season with the black pepper, cool to room temperature and serve immediately.

Apricot & pesto tarts

After a visit to New York, a friend raved about a superb starter she'd had at a bistro. I just had to try my hand. At the last tasting, she declared that I'd just about got it right!

- 50 ml melted butter
- 30 apricot halves – fresh or tinned
- 25 g castor sugar
- 4 sheets phyllo pastry
- 250 ml fresh pesto

Preheat the oven to 180 deg C/Gas 4. Butter a baking sheet with 20 g of the butter. Place the apricot halves on the sheet, sprinkle with the castor sugar, and bake for 25 minutes until slightly caramelised.

Use the rest of the melted butter to lightly paint the phyllo pastry sheets, and cut each sheet into 6 squares. Fold the squares into six small flan pans (use 4 squares per tartlet). Spoon a dollop of pesto into each phyllo case and place 5 apricot halves, bottoms up, on top of the pesto. Pop back into the oven for 20 minutes or until the phyllo turns a light caramel colour. Serve as a starter with a green salad tossed in a light walnut oil dressing.

Fromage de chèvre on toast with salad

Serves 6

Goat's milk cheese, or fromage de chèvre, as the French call it, is fast becoming a must do for cooks – and a must order when you see it on a menu!

- 6 slices fresh rye bread
- 6 T olive oil
- 125 g basil pesto
- 6 slices goat's cheese
- soft green salad leaves, mixed with small tomatoes
- 6 T walnut oil

Place the bread on a pan, and spoon the olive oil over. Drop a dollop of pesto on each slice before adding the cheese. Quick-grill the bread and cheese. Toss the leaves and tomatoes with walnut oil, place the slices on top, and serve.

Onion tart with cheese & apple cider glaze

Serves 4

This freeform tart really tastes as good as it looks. Enjoy!

- 1 sheet puff pastry
- 125 ml apple cider
- 50 g castor sugar
- 15 g butter
- 15 small onions, peeled and halved
- 1 T dried sweet basil
- 125 g mozzarella, grated
- 125 g Gruyère, grated
- 4 sprigs fresh thyme, shredded

Preheat the oven to 220 deg C/Gas 7. Roll out the pastry on a lightly buttered baking tray. In a medium-sized saucepan, bring the apple cider to a slow boil. Melt the sugar and butter in the cider before adding the onions and basil. Cook until the cider has almost evaporated and the onions are lightly caramelised.

Sprinkle the grated cheeses onto the pastry, spoon the onion mixture evenly on top, and use the remaining cider, sugar and butter syrup to glaze. Add the thyme, and tuck the pastry around the onions before baking for about 30 minutes.

Serve with a green salad.

Green beans with anchovies & almonds

We all need to eat our greens. This is a good way to do just that.

- 300 g fine green beans, topped
- 50 ml olive oil
- 6 anchovies
- 3 cloves garlic, finely chopped
- 125 g almonds, slivered and roasted

Quickly boil the beans for about 4 minutes. Drain and keep warm. Heat the olive oil and anchovies in a small pan until the anchovies have melted away. Remove from the heat and add the garlic. Let it warm thoroughly.

Spoon this sauce over the beans, sprinkle with almonds and serve as a great side dish to any meat. This is brilliant with lamb!

Chapter 6

In front of the fireplace

On a rainy Cape winter's day, this is where you'll find me, cuddled up with a book. My new pair of glasses will be balanced precariously on the tip of my nose, and there will be a glass of red wine close at hand. The small table in front of the fireplace is the perfect size for a meal for two, and on it, you'll find pot pies, toasted tomatoes with Gorgonzola, bowls of lentils, or potato and leek soup ... I love winter afternoons.

Lentil & mushroom soup

Lentils have a dull-but-worthy reputation. It's time to get over that. This soup is amazing – and puy lentils are increasingly easy to find.

- 1 onion, finely chopped
- 100 ml duck fat or olive oil
- 2 cloves garlic, chopped
- 1 large potato, peeled and diced
- 600 g mushrooms, chopped into tiny pieces
- 300 g puy lentils, simmered in 600 ml water until tender (about 30 min)
- 500 ml chicken stock
- sea salt and freshly ground black pepper

Sauté the onion in fat or oil for 3 to 4 minutes. Add the garlic, potato and mushrooms, cover, and sweat for a few minutes. Stir well. When the lentils are tender, tip the mushroom mixture into the lentil pot and add the stock. Bring to a simmer and season. Blend the soup with a handheld blender. Reheat and serve very hot with persillade or a dollop of tapenade.

Potato & leek soup

When served cold, this soup is better known as vichyssoise. It was first made in America by a French chef who hailed from Vichy in the Auvergne.

- 6 leeks, green leaves discarded
- 60 g salted butter
- 6 to 8 potatoes, peeled and chopped roughly
- 1½ ℓ chicken stock
- 250 ml double cream
- salt and freshly ground black pepper to taste
- olive oil and sprigs fresh thyme to garnish

First slice the leeks in thin rounds before rinsing them thoroughly. Heat the butter in a heavy-based saucepan and fry the leeks until softened. Add the potatoes and chicken stock and bring to the boil. Add some water if you think it is necessary. Reduce the heat and let it simmer until the potatoes are soft. Liquidise the soup until it is smooth and creamy, return to the saucepan and reheat gently, adding the cream.

Season to taste and serve garnished with a dribble of olive oil and a sprig of thyme.

English pot pies à la David

Jellied stock

- 3 or 4 medium-sized pork trotters
- trimmings from the pork belly
- 1 onion, peeled and chopped
- 1 carrot, peeled and sliced
- 1 bay leaf
- a little parsley, roughly chopped
- salt and freshly ground pepper

Basic pork pie mix

- 14 g butter
- 1 onion, finely chopped
- 1 t each of fresh sage, fresh thyme and ground mace
- 1 t each of dry mustard and mixed spice
- 455 g pork belly, weighed without skin or bones
- coarsely ground salt and pepper

Pastry

- 170 g flour
- pinch salt
- 90 ml milk and 90 ml water
- 85 g lard

Jellied stock

Place all the ingredients in a pot, cover with water and simmer for about 2 hours. Sieve, season with salt and pepper, and reduce further until it forms a jelly when cold.

Basic pork pie mix

Put all ingredients through a coarse grinder.

Pastry

Sift the flour and salt into a bowl, and make a well in the centre.

Place the milk and lard into a saucepan, melt the lard, and bring the mixture to a boil. Pour into the flour, working very quickly with a wooden spoon. Knead by hand to produce a smooth dough with a texture like putty.

Line twelve 7 cm x 5 cm deep moulds while the pastry is still warm.

To assemble

Preheat the oven to 200 deg C/Gas 6. Fill the pastry moulds with pork pie mix to about 5 mm of the rim. Bake for about an hour or until the pastry is browned. Spoon the warm jellied stock over to cover. Top with any one of the following, and leave to cool: cranberry sauce, onion confit, mild blue cheese or chutney.

Toasted tomatoes with pesto & Gorgonzola

Serves 6

Shared with family and friends this is great as a snack, as a starter or as a light meal served with a large salad.

- 6 plum tomatoes, halved
- salt and freshly ground black pepper
- 150 ml olive oil
- 200 g Gorgonzola, crumbled
- 12 slices of baguette, lightly toasted
- 125 ml basil pesto
- basil leaves to serve

Place the tomato halves on an oiled baking tray. Season lightly and drizzle a little olive oil over them. Grill for about 5 minutes before adding a sprinkling of Gorgonzola over each tomato. Return to the oven and allow the cheese to melt and cook slightly.

Arrange the little toasted slices of bread on individual plates, and place the hot tomatoes on top. Spoon a teaspoon of pesto on top of each one. Scatter the basil leaves over them and dress with the rest of the olive oil and a little black pepper.

Serve immediately.

French onion tart

I regularly serve this as a starter ... paired with a glass of Sémillon.

- 1 sheet puff pastry
- 1 kg brown onions, peeled and chopped
- 25 ml olive oil
- 1 T butter
- 5 rashers bacon, diced
- 1 T thyme leaves
- 1 T flour
- 300 ml thick cream
- 2 eggs
- 2 egg yolks
- salt and freshly ground black pepper

Preheat the oven to 180 deg C/Gas 4. Press the pastry into a 25 cm lightly greased flan ring with your fingertips. Lift the pastry up the side of the pan. Keep in the fridge until needed.

In a frying pan, fry the onions over a low heat in the olive oil and butter until they turn a beautiful golden brown. Add the bacon and thyme. Sprinkle with flour and, over a low heat, stir in the cream. Keep stirring until the mixture has turned quite creamy. Remove from the heat.

Beat the eggs and egg yolks together, and fold them into the mixture. Season to taste and spread over the pastry base. Cook the tart in the oven for about 40 minutes. Once the tart is cooked, allow it to rest a little before serving.

Grilled prawns with limes

A delightfully easy recipe.

- 16 large prawns
- juice of 3 limes
- 3 cloves garlic, peeled and crushed
- 2 red chillies, chopped
- salt and freshly ground black pepper

Clean the prawns without peeling them. In a bowl, mix together the lime juice, garlic and chillies. Season to taste, and toss the prawns in the marinade. Leave to soak for 30 minutes.

Place the prawns under a hot grill for about 2 minutes before turning them over to cook for 2 more minutes. Serve immediately with some extra limes and fresh chillies.

Beef burger

There is no reason why a burger has to be junk food.

- 1 kg shredded steak
- 1 onion, peeled and finely chopped
- olive oil
- pinch cumin seeds
- 1 T coriander seeds
- sea salt and freshly ground black pepper
- handful freshly grated Parmesan
- 1 heaped T English mustard
- 1 large free-range egg

Put the meat in a bowl. In a large frying pan, slowly cook the onion in a little olive oil for about 5 minutes, and then mix it with the shredded meat. Using a mortar and pestle, grind the cumin and coriander seeds with a pinch of salt and freshly ground pepper until fine, and add it to the meat mixture. Then add the Parmesan, mustard and egg. Mix well. Shape the patties and place them on grease-proof paper. Chill in the fridge for about 1 hour.

When the condiments are ready, heat a pan, add some olive oil and gently fry the patties until they are cooked to your liking. Serve immediately with a dollop of guacamole. This is delicious!

Homemade mayonnaise

Makes about 350 ml

What would we do without good mayonnaise in the kitchen?

- 2 egg yolks
- 10 ml creamy mustard
- sea salt and freshly ground black pepper
- 250 ml extra virgin olive oil
- 5 ml lemon juice

Whisk together the egg yolks, mustard and a little pinch of salt and pepper. Pour the oil in slowly in a thin and steady stream, whisking continuously at a gentle pace. When all the ingredients have been incorporated, whisk more vigorously to make a thick mayonnaise.* Add the lemon juice and whisk.

* *If at this point you add the pulp of 3 garlic cloves to the mayonnaise, you will have a superb aioli to serve with soups or vegetables.*

Chunky guacamole

- 2 large avocados, just ripe
- 1 T onion, finely chopped
- 1 chilli, thinly sliced
- 1 large tomato, unpeeled and finely chopped
- 2 sprigs coriander, chopped
- lime juice
- salt

Halve the avocados, and remove the pips and skin. With a fork, mash the flesh, leaving it fairly chunky. In a bowl, combine the avocados, onion, chilli, tomato and coriander, and mix gently using a spoon. Add a few drops of lime juice and salt to taste. Serve immediately.

Skate with black butter & capers

This is a regular dish in French country kitchens. I love it.

- 2 leeks
- 1 bouquet garni
- 2 celery stalks
- 1,5 kg skate wings
- 150 g butter
- juice from 1 lemon
- 2 T capers
- salt and pepper

Prepare a vegetable stock by simmering 1 ℓ of water with the leeks, bouquet garni and celery for 1 hour. Poach the skate for 10 minutes in the stock, remove, and scoop the flesh from the fish bones … It is relatively easy.

Melt the butter over a gentle heat and cook until it develops a beautiful golden colour. Add the lemon juice and capers, and season. Dress the skate with the melted caper butter.

Chapter 7

In the kitchen

Kitchen lunches must be a favourite memory of all food lovers. Where else do you throw yourself into a chair, wine glass in hand, and watch a friend busy herself with your meal? There is no better place or time to discuss the merits of this deli versus that, this cut of meat or that. Nobody will notice as you naughtily cut the tip off the Gorgonzola just to pair it with the wine in your glass ... or as you 'taste' a gently stock-broiled marrow bone, sucking noisily ... or as you pick toasted pine nuts out of the pan. Kitchen eating is best.

Mushroom soup with tapenade

If you've just come in from a long walk with sea spray blowing in your face, this is what you will need!

- 75 ml butter
- 500 g brown mushrooms, sliced
- 1 ℓ chicken stock
- 2 cloves garlic, peeled
- 250 ml thick cream
- salt to taste
- freshly ground black pepper to taste
- 30 ml crème fraîche
- 50 g tapenade

Melt the butter in a soup pot. Wait for it to brown before adding the mushrooms. Fry the mushrooms over a high heat until the juices have cooked away, before adding the chicken stock. Bring to a rapid boil. Add the garlic.

Reduce the heat and simmer until the liquid has been reduced by half. Remove from the heat and liquidise.

Return the thick soup to the pot and reheat gently.

Remove from the heat, fold in the cream, season and spoon into warmed soup plates. Drop a dollop of crème fraîche into the middle of each plate, followed by a spoonful of tapenade. Serve immediately – it's absolutely heart-warming with fresh crusty bread!

French onion soup

A typical French soup, without any extras ... just as it should be.

- 6 large brown onions, peeled and thinly sliced
- 50 g butter
- 25 g flour
- 2 T fresh thyme leaves, stripped from their stems
- 2 cloves garlic, chopped
- 2 ℓ good chicken stock
- salt to taste
- 3 T port

To serve
- 8 slices of white baguette
- 200 g Gruyère, grated

Fry the onions in the butter without allowing them to brown. When they are gloriously translucent with a subtle hint of caramel, sprinkle with the flour. Add the thyme. Continue cooking for a minute or two, stirring with a wooden spoon. Add the garlic. Gradually pour the stock over the onions, stirring gently. Continue to cook for another 30 minutes over a gentle heat. Season, and flavour the delicious soup with the port. In the meantime, switch on your oven's grill, cover the slices of baguette generously with the Gruyère, and toast until meltingly hot. To serve, ladle the steaming soup into soup bowls and float a Gruyère toast on top. Utterly sumptuous!

Mozzarella salad with anchovies & capers

Serves 2

Utterly simple and utterly unforgettable.

- 250 g fresh buffalo mozzarella
- 2 T extra virgin olive oil
- 1 t well-aged balsamic vinegar
- 1 t excellent mustard ... I'm really partial to the mustard from Charroux
- 1 T small capers
- 6 small white anchovies
- 1 T fennel leaves, finely chopped
- sea salt and freshly ground black pepper to taste

Allow the buffalo mozzarella to rest outside the fridge until it reaches room temperature. In a small bowl, lightly whisk the olive oil, balsamic vinegar and mustard together. Toss the capers into the vinaigrette. Using your fingers, shred the mozzarella onto a serving dish, and spoon the caper mixture over the cheese. Arrange the white anchovies prettily on top and lightly garnish with the chopped fennel leaves. Season to taste and serve with a piece of warm, crusty bread and a glass of white wine.

Gnocchi with green olives & Gorgonzola cream

Serves 6 as a starter portion

I love serving this on big old china plates around our kitchen table with crusty bread and lots of red wine.

- 50 ml olive oil
- 1 red-skinned onion, peeled and chopped
- 100 g green olives, stoned
- 250 ml chicken stock
- 250 ml cream
- 125 g creamy Gorgonzola
- 5 ml coarse salt
- 500 g gnocchi
- 18 anchovies, drained
- 25 g salad onion, chopped

Heat the olive oil in a pot, add the onion and gently fry it before adding the olives.

Pour the chicken stock into the pot, bring to the boil and reduce by half. Add the cream and the Gorgonzola, and gently stir until the cheese has melted. Remove from the heat.

Bring 2 ℓ of water to the boil in a pasta pot and add the salt. Drop in the gnocchi, and scoop them out as soon as they rise to the top. Drop them directly on the warmed pasta plates.

In the meantime, reheat the sauce and add the anchovies. Spoon over the gnocchi. Sprinkle each dish with chopped salad onions and serve immediately.

Marrow bones on toast

What is life without the marrow?
Serve with a flourish and a glass of
robust red!

- 12 thick-cut marrow bones
- 1 *ℓ* chicken stock
- 12 slices white bread
- salt and freshly ground black
  pepper

Put the marrow bones on their sides in a pot – that way the marrow won't fall out during cooking. Cover with water and bring to the boil. Boil the bones for about 5 minutes, then pour the water off. Refill the pot with fresh water, and bring to the boil again. Repeat the process once more, but the third time, rather than water, pour the chicken stock over the bones and bring to the boil. Boil for 10 minutes, then remove the bones from the pot, leaving the stock to reduce. Remove the pot from the heat once the stock has been reduced by three quarters.

Toast the bread, and arrange two slices each on a small plate. Spoon the marrow on top, and pour some of the reduced stock over. Season to taste and serve immediately.

Butternut & chèvre tartlets with pine nuts

A match made in heaven. And do add the chilli.

- 1 roll puff pastry, thawed
- 1 egg white
- 50 ml olive oil
- 6 leeks, sliced into pennies and rinsed
- 1 red chilli, chopped
- 6 x 5 mm-thick slices butternut, oven-baked
- 6 slices chèvre
- 12 sage leaves
- salt and freshly ground black pepper
- crème fraîche
- pine nuts, lightly toasted

Preheat the oven to 220 deg C/Gas 7. Line 6 oiled tart ramekins with pastry. Prick with a fork and brush with egg white.

Warm the olive oil in a pan, and fry the leeks and chilli until translucent but not browned.

Remove from the heat and allow to cool. Spoon into the tart bases, cover with a slice of butternut, follow with a slice of chèvre, and garnish with sage leaves. Season to taste and bake for about 15 minutes.

Serve with a small dollop of seasoned crème fraîche and a sprinkle of pine nuts.

These little tartlets are delightful with chilled Sémillon.

Chapter 8

Around the yellowwood table

Our ancient yellowwood table is a thing of great beauty. On it, we have noisy family lunches, plate to wood, not a tablecloth in sight! We put whole bread on planks and serve wonderful meals to the masses of uncles, aunts, cousins and grandparents. There might be bowls of venison on pasta, roasted pears with chicken breast salad, and, of course, delicious soups. There will certainly be lots of talking, laughter and fabulous Cape wines. Tables must be able to tell wonderful stories.

Cauliflower soup with truffle oil

I was inspired by John Burton Race's
French Leave programme on BBC
— it's superb!

- 100 g salted butter
- 1 kg fresh cauliflower, trimmed
  and broken into florets
- 3 leeks, peeled, chopped and
  rinsed
- 4 cloves garlic, chopped
- 3 sprigs fresh thyme, plus an
  extra sprig per serving for
  garnish
- 2 bay leaves
- 800 ml chicken stock
- 125 ml full cream
- truffle oil

Melt the butter in a soup pot and add the cauliflower florets,
stirring them into the butter.

Add the leeks, garlic, thyme and bay leaves, and fry
lightly. Add stock to the vegetables and bring to a slow,
pleasant boil. Keep this going until the cauliflower is soft.
Remove the bay leaves and thyme sprigs from the pot, and
liquidise the soup. Reheat gently, stir in the cream, spoon
into lovely, large soup plates, and add a drop of truffle oil
to each. Garnish with a sprig of thyme, and serve this gor-
geous soup with some crusty bread.

Smoked oyster soup

This is a very fast, fabulous, cheap soup – ideal for an emergency!

- 1 tin mushroom soup, preferably Campbell's
- 1 tin smoked oysters
- 250 ml double cream
- 50 ml dry sherry
- 50 g flat-leaf parsley, chopped
- freshly ground black pepper

Heat the soup in a small saucepan. Halve the oysters and add, along with the cream and sherry. Stir gently whilst heating the soup. Do not boil. Spoon into warmed soup bowls and garnish with the parsley after a nice, solid grind of the pepper mill ... voila! Serve with a slice of crusty brown bread.

Roasted pears with asparagus & green beans

This salad is a firm favourite during summer lunches as either a starter, or served after the main course.

- 3 firm, ripe pears
- 100 ml extra virgin olive oil
- 20 g castor sugar
- 600 g young green beans, topped and tailed
- 30 green asparagus spears
- 100 g walnuts, roasted and chopped

Dressing
- 50 ml walnut oil
- 50 ml cream
- 1 t smooth mustard
- 1 clove garlic, peeled and finely chopped
- salt and pepper to taste

Preheat the oven to 180 deg C/Gas 4. Halve the pears, skin on, and cut each half into thirds. Line up the pear slices in a roasting pan, drizzle with 30 ml olive oil and sprinkle the castor sugar over evenly. Bake for 20 minutes until the pears have coloured slightly but are still crunchy.

Meanwhile, pour a little cold water into a shallow frying pan. Add the beans and the asparagus, and bring to a gentle, happy boil. Do not cover – this will help to retain the bright green of the vegetables. Remove from the heat after 5 minutes – the vegetables must still be crunchy. Drain and immediately toss 20 ml olive oil into the warm beans and asparagus. Season lightly.

In the meantime, make the creamy vinaigrette dressing by shaking together the remaining olive oil, the walnut oil, the cream, mustard, garlic, and salt and pepper.

Allow the beans, asparagus and pears to cool. Add the walnuts and vinaigrette, and toss the salad. Serve.

Smoked chicken breast salad

Serves 8 as a starter

You should also try this with duck – a stunner!

- 10 sprigs fresh thyme
- 10 fresh sage leaves
- freshly ground black pepper
- 2 whole smoked chicken breasts
- 50 ml olive oil
- 2 punnets rocket leaves
- 20 basil leaves

Vinaigrette
- 150 ml extra virgin olive oil
- juice of ½ lemon
- 50 ml castor sugar
- 5 ml creamy mustard
- sea salt and freshly ground black pepper

Chop the thyme and sage and, in a small bowl, mix the herbs with the pepper.

Using your fingers, rub the herb mixture into the chicken breasts. Heat the olive oil in a warm saucepan. Put the breasts into the pan and fry the meat very lightly just to release the different herb flavours.

Remove the breasts from the heat and slice in thin slivers. Toss the rocket, basil and vinaigrette together before arranging a little heap in the centre of each plate. Add the chicken slices and serve.

Vinaigrette
Pour the olive oil and lemon juice into a mixing bowl. Add the sugar and mustard, and whisk the vinaigrette until the sugar has dissolved. Season to taste and toss with the salad leaves.

Venison tagliatelle

This recipe is firmly aimed at the hunters among us who love to use every bit of the tasty meat.

- 8 whole tomatoes, peeled and puréed
- 1 T fresh oregano, chopped
- 1 T fresh basil, chopped
- 1 T fresh parsley, chopped
- 2 cloves garlic, chopped
- sea salt and freshly ground black pepper
- 500 g fresh tagliatelle
- 100 ml olive oil
- 500 g fynvleis or rillette*
- 250 ml crème fraîche
- 125 ml quince jelly

Stew the tomatoes in a large pot over a low heat for about 20 minutes, or until thickened. Stir in the herbs and garlic, and simmer for another minute or two. Season to taste. Remove from the heat.

Cook the pasta in plenty of boiling, salted water until al dente. Drain and toss with a little of the olive oil.

Heat the rest of the oil over high heat in a large frying pan. Add the fynvleis, season to taste and fry until heated through – about 3 minutes. Reduce the heat and fold in the tomato sauce.

Serve the pasta in large bowls. Spoon the ragout on top of the pasta, finish off with a dollop of crème fraîche and serve the quince jelly on the side.

Tremendous food this!

* *To make fynvleis or rillette, take all the bones you can lay your hands on and place them in your biggest pot. I have an ancient 34 ℓ Rosieres, which is perfect. Add dry white wine to just about cover the bones, a handful of garlic cloves, a handful of rosemary, parsley and chives, and about 10 leeks. Also into the pot go some bay leaves, a couple of sprigs of thyme, 1 T dried coriander, 1 t juniper berries and about 500 ml olive oil. And to add interest, I throw in about 4 pork trotters.*

Cover the pot and leave it in peace to simmer away for at least 4 hours, topping up with more dry white if needed. At the end of the cooking time, scoop the bones into a large

continues overleaf

dish (leave the juices simmering) and separate the meat. Do it by hand (gloves do come in handy). While you're doing this, the amazing stock is reducing to a wonderfully rich sauce.

Spoon the meat into plastic bags, each with a ladle or two of sauce which, when it cools, becomes a delicious jelly. Freeze what you don't use immediately. Fantastic for instant venison pie or, as here, ragout for pasta.

Blue cheese tart with phyllo pastry

This tart was first made for me years ago as a light supper before a rather weighty opera, and I've never quite gotten over it.

- 10 ml butter, melted
- 4 sheets phyllo pastry
- 2 celery sticks, thinly chopped
- 250 g Roquefort, crumbled
- 125 ml cream
- 2 eggs, whisked
- freshly ground black pepper to taste

Preheat the oven to 180 deg C/Gas 4. Brush the melted butter gently over the sheets of phyllo. Place the sheets, one on top of the other at an angle, in a buttered tart dish.

Fry the celery in a little leftover butter until it is lightly cooked. Remove the pan from the heat, and stir the cheese, cream, eggs and pepper into the celery.

Pour the mixture into the phyllo pastry case and, using your fingers, mould the pastry to your liking ... prettily or artistically! ... before putting it in the oven for around 35 minutes, or until the phyllo turns a light caramel colour and the filling has set. Serve warm with rocket and a dollop of quince jelly.

Index

French onion soup 130

La soupe des vendanges 56

Lentil & mushroom soup 106

Mushroom soup 16

Mushroom soup with tapenade 128

Potato & leek soup 108

Smoked oyster soup 144

Spinach & sorrel soup 38

Tomato, chickpea & lentil soup 74

Tarts & pies

Apricot & pesto tarts 96

Blue cheese tart with phyllo pastry 154

Butternut & chèvre tartlets with pine nuts 138

Classic quiche Lorraine 72

English pot pies à la David 110

French onion tart 114

Fromage de chèvre on toast with salad 98

Fromage de chèvre tartlets 26

Goat's cheese tarts with hazelnuts 46

Onion tart with cheese & apple cider glaze 100

Pissaladière 66

Provençal vegetable tart 52

Terrine de Campagne 28

Tomato tarts 62

Glossary

aioli: garlic mayonnaise

al dente: still slightly chewy; not too soft

baguette: flute-shaped loaf of French bread

bain-marie: pan with simmering water with a bowl suspended in it

beurre noisette: butter that has been gently heated in a frying pan until it is a dark golden colour and gives off a nutty smell

bouquet garni: selection of aromatic herbs and plants, tied together in a small bundle and used to add flavour to sauces and stocks

braise: to lightly brown in fat and then cook slowly with a lid on in a small amount of liquid

brocante: antique market

canapé: small piece of bread or toast with a savoury topping

caramelise: to convert into a caramel-like consistency

carpaccio: Italian dish made of paper-thin slices of beef, dressed with olive oil and Parmesan

chèvre: cheese made from goat's milk

cognac: world-famous brandy distilled from wine, made in the region of Cognac in France

compote: fruit stewed with sugar or in a syrup

confit: piece of meat cooked in its own fat and stored; covered in its own fat to preserve it

crème fraîche: cream to which a lactic acid has been added that thickens the cream and gives it a distinctive sharp flavour without souring the cream

crudités: selection of vegetables served as an appetiser with a dip

de campagne: countryside

daube: beef dish cooked in a casserole, usually with wine

dollop: scoop

flambée: to flame with cognac or other alcohol

fromage de chèvre: goat's milk cheese

glaze: to cover with a shiny coating

gnocchi: kind of dumpling closely linked to pasta, made either from pasta dough or from a mixture of potato flour and wheat flour; the Roman homemade kind is made from a boiled potato and egg mixture

hazelnut oil: can be replaced with extra virgin olive oil

horseradish cream: condiment belonging to the crucifer family, grated and made into a sauce with cream and/or egg; often with lemon juice; served with beef and fish

infuse(ion): process of steeping an aromatic substance in a boiling liquid until the liquid has absorbed the flavour

pancetta: cured, unsmoked pork belly that is rolled and tied

pâté: spread of finely minced meat

persillade: mixture of chopped parsley and garlic

pissaladière: French type of pizza

poach: lightly boil in wine or water

pot-au-feu: dish symbolic of French cuisine and a meal in itself; various meats cooked lengthily in water with vegetables and served at the same time as a meal; dish of different meats, placed on a platter and sliced separately, and the broth is eaten

prosciutto: Italian word for ham, usually referring to the raw hams of Parma in Italy

pulse: intermittent beating (as in 'mix')

purée: creaming cooked foods through a sieve or with a food processor

ragout: stew made from meat, poultry, game, fish or vegetables that is cooked in a thickened liquid and flavoured with herbs and seasoning

ramekin: small ovenproof mould

reduce: to concentrate or thicken a sauce or soup by boiling

rillette: preparation of pork, rabbit, goose, game or poultry, deboned and cooked in lard, and then

pounded to a smooth paste, potted and served as a cold snack

sauté: to cook meat, fish or vegetables in fat until brown

stock: flavoured liquid base for making a sauce, stew or braised dish

strain: to filter through either a strainer, colander or cloth

sweat: to cook vegetables in fat over a gentle heat so that they become soft and their juices are concentrated in the cooking fat

tagliolini: flat ribbon pasta, narrower than tagliatelle

tapenade: paste made of cured black olives, seasoned with olive oil, garlic, anchovies, capers and lemon

terrine: mix of chopped vegetables, meats and flavourings pressed into a container, cooked and served cold

vichyssoise: leek and potato soup thickened with fresh cream and served cold

vinaigrette: dressing made from oil, vinegar and seasoning

walnut oil: can be replaced with extra virgin olive oil

zest: coloured or outer rind of any citrus fruit